ANIMALS *in* DANGER

Cheetah

Rod Theodorou

Heinemann Library
Chicago, Illinois

© 2001 Reed Educational & Professional Publishing
Published by Heinemann Library,
an imprint of Reed Educational & Professional Publishing,
Chicago, IL

Customer Service 888-454-2279

Visit our website at www.heinemannlibrary.com

Designed by Ron Kamen
Illustrations by Dewi Morris/Robert Sydenham
Originated by Ambassador Litho Ltd.
Printed in China

08 07
10 9 8 7 6 5 4 3

Library of Congress Cataloging-in-Publication Data
Theodorou, Rod.
    Cheetah / Rod Theodorou.
      p. cm. -- (Animals in danger)
    Includes bibliographical references and index (p.).
    ISBN 1-57572-269-0 (lib. bdg.)   ISBN 1-58810-363-3 (pbk. bdg.)
    ISBN 978-1-57572-269-6 (lib. bdg.)   ISBN 978-1-58810-363-5 (pbk. bdg.)
     1. Cheetah--Juvenile literature. 2. Endangered species--Juvenile literature. [1. Cheetah.
  2. Endangered species.] I. Title.

QL737.C23 T4734 2001
599.75'9--dc21   00-063264

Acknowledgments
The author and publishers are grateful to the following for permission to reproduce copyright material: Heather Angel, p. 27; Ardea, p. 4: Ardea/Ferrero-Labat, pp. 11, 13; Ardea/Francois Gohier, p. 4; Ardea/Martin W. Grosnick, p. 6; Ardea/Clem Haagner, pp. 17, 21; Ardea/Chris Harvey, p. 9; BBC/ Karl Amman, p. 18; BBC/Peter Blackwell, p. 14, BBC/Eliot Lyons, p. 16; BBC/Peter Oxford, p. 15; BBC/Anup Shah, p. 20; Bruce Coleman/Gerald S. Cubitt, p. 26; Bruce Coleman/John Shaw, p. 4; Bruce Coleman/Gunter Ziesler, p. 7; FLPA/Frants Hartmann, p. 22, FLPA/Fritz Polking, p. 23; FLPA/N. B. Wither, p. 19; Natural Science Photos, p. 25; NHPA/Martin Wendler, p. 24; WWF Photolibrary/Martin Harvey, p. 8; WWF Photolibrary/Denis Huot, p. 5; WWF Photolibrary/Fritz Polking, p. 12.

Cover photograph reproduced with permission of Still Pictures.

Some words are shown in bold, **like this.** You can find out what they mean by looking in the glossary.

Contents

Animals in Danger

leatherback sea turtle

koala

polar bear

All over the world, more than 25,000 animal **species** are in danger. Some are in danger because their homes are being destroyed. Many are in danger because people hunt them.

This book is about cheetahs and why they are
endangered. Unless people learn to **protect** them,
cheetahs will become **extinct**. We will only be
able to find out about them from books like this.

What Are Cheetahs?

Cheetahs are **mammals.** They are members of the big cat family. Cheetahs are not as large as other big cats such as lions, tigers, and leopards.

Cheetahs are a special **species** of big cat. They are built to run amazingly fast. They can run faster than any other animal on Earth!

What Do Cheetahs Look Like?

Cheetahs are built to run. They have thin **muscular** bodies and small heads. They have long strong legs and long, **flexible** backs.

Unlike all other cats, cheetahs have claws that cannot be pulled back into their paws. The claws act like spikes on running shoes. They help the cheetahs run fast.

Where Do Cheetahs Live?

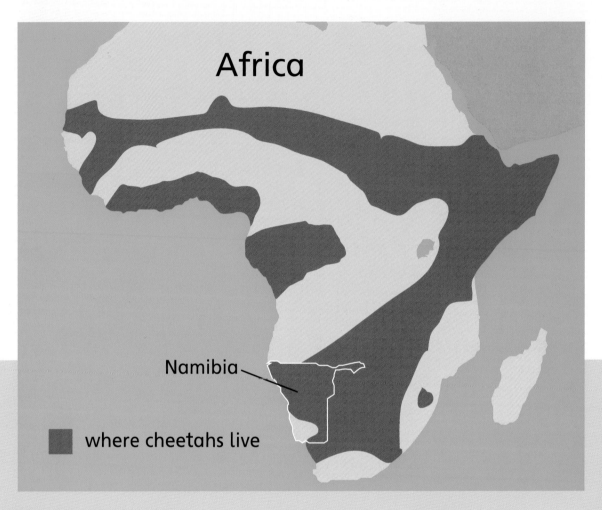

Africa

Namibia

where cheetahs live

Cheetahs live in many countries in Africa. The largest **population** of cheetahs lives in the African country of Namibia.

Cheetahs like to live in open spaces, like grasslands or **savannah,** where they can easily see their **prey** and enemies. Some cheetahs live in more mountainous areas.

What Do Cheetahs Eat?

Cheetahs are **carnivores**. They **stalk** their **prey** for a long time. They wait until there is about the length of a school bus between them and their prey. Then they suddenly run after it.

Cheetahs hunt small prey, such as rabbits or game birds. Sometimes they hunt medium-sized prey, like small antelope. They bite the neck of the animal to kill it.

Cheetah Babies

Female cheetahs give birth to a **litter** of four to five cubs. The mother hides them in tall grass. Lions or hyenas will kill cheetah cubs if they find them.

The cubs have long hairs running down their backs. These hairs **camouflage** the cubs when they are hiding in tall grass.

Caring for the Cubs

The mother has to leave the cubs when it is time for her to go hunting. When the cubs are six weeks old, they start to follow her and learn how to hunt.

After eighteen months the mother leaves her cubs to live alone. The **males** stay together and help each other hunt, but soon the **females** wander off and live alone.

Unusual Cheetah Facts

Cheetahs can run as fast as a car driving on the highway! They can only run this fast for about twenty seconds, then they start to get very tired.

The Egyptian **pharaohs** thought that cheetahs were a special royal animal. They caught them in the wild and used them to hunt other animals. They also kept them as pets.

How Many Cheetahs Are There?

Thousands of years ago cheetahs lived in many countries all over the world. Now there are only small **populations** left.

In 1960, there were about 56,000 cheetahs left. Today there may be as few as 15,000. In Iran there are only about 100 cheetahs left.

Why Is the Cheetah in Danger?

Cheetahs need very large areas to live in. More and more of their land is being turned into farmland. This leaves less **prey** for the cheetahs.

Sometimes a cheetah will attack a farmer's cattle. Farmers kill many cheetahs by setting traps for them or shooting them.

Poachers also shoot cheetahs for their beautiful spotted fur. The furs are often sold to make coats and rugs.

As their land disappears, the cheetahs find it harder to hide from their enemies. Lions and hyenas attack them, steal their food, and kill many of their cubs.

How Is the Cheetah Being Helped?

Selling cheetah fur is now **illegal**. **Conservation** groups such as the World Wildlife Fund are working to stop **poaching** and save the cheetah.

Unfortunately, cheetahs do not survive well in **game reserves** because they have to share the land with lions and hyenas. They rarely **breed** in captivity.

Cheetah Fact File

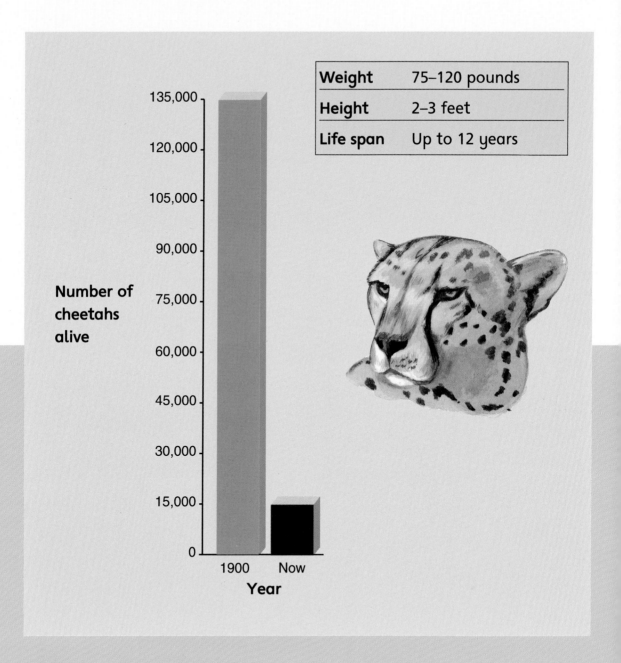

Weight	75–120 pounds
Height	2–3 feet
Life span	Up to 12 years

Number of cheetahs alive

135,000
120,000
105,000
90,000
75,000
60,000
45,000
30,000
15,000
0

1900   Now

Year

World Danger Table

	Number when animal was listed as endangered	Number that may be alive today
Cheetah	1,500–3,000	15,000
Cougar	2,000	4,000–6,000
Leopard	The leopard is not endangered.	up to 700,000
Lion	The lion is not endangered.	about 100,000
Tiger	1,800–4,000	5,000–7,000

There are many other animals in the world that are in danger of becoming **extinct**. This table shows some big cats that are in danger.

How Can You Help the Cheetah?

If you and your friends raise money for the cheetahs, you can send it to these organizations. They take the money and use it to pay conservation workers and to buy food and tools to help save the cheetah.

Cheetah Conservation Fund/WILD
P.O. Box 1380
Ojai, CA 93024

Defenders of Wildlife
1101 Fourteenth St., N.W. #1400
Washington, DC 20005

World Wildlife Fund
1250 Twenty-fourth St.
P.O. Box 97180
Washington, DC 20037

More Books to Read

Dupont, Philippe. *The Cheetah*. Charlesbridge Publishing, 1992.

Juster Esbensen, Barbara. *Swift As The Wind*. Orchard Books, 1996.

Morrison, Taylor. *Cheetah*. New York: Henry Holt & Company, 1998.

Glossary

breed to have babies

camouflage to be colored or shaped like the place you live so you are hidden and hard to see

captivity kept by people and not living free in the wild

carnivore animal that eats only meat

conservation looking after things, especially if they are in danger

endangered group of animals that is dying out, so there are few left

extinct group of animals that has completely died out and can never live again

female girl or woman

flexible bends easily

game wild animals

illegal against the law

male boy or man

mammal animal with hair, like a human, that drinks its mother's milk as a baby

muscular to have strong muscles

pharaoh ruler in ancient Egypt

poacher hunter who makes money from hunting animals to sell parts of their bodies such as teeth and fur

population total number of animals in a place

prey animals that are hunted and killed by other animals

protect keep safe

reserve large area where animals are looked after by guards

savannah large areas in hot countries covered by grass and very few trees

species group of living things that are very similar

stalk to watch and carefully follow

Index